HUMAN
BODY

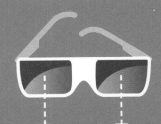

50
SCIENCE
EXPERIMENTS
TO MAKE AND DO

Silver Dolphin

Silver Dolphin Books

An imprint of Printers Row Publishing Group
A division of Readerlink Distribution Services, LLC
10350 Barnes Canyon Road, Suite 100, San Diego, CA 92121
www.silverdolphinbooks.com

Written by Sally MacGill
Illustrated by Adam Linley, Daniel Sanchez Limon,
Keri Green, and Martyn Cain/Beehive Illustration

Printers Row Publishing Group is a division of
Readerlink Distribution Services, LLC.
Silver Dolphin Books is a registered trademark of
Readerlink Distribution Services, LLC.

All notations of errors or omissions should be addressed to
Silver Dolphin Books, Editorial
Department, at the above address. All other correspondence
(author inquiries, permissions)
concerning the content of this book should be addressed to
Quarto Children's Books Ltd,
The Old Brewery, 6 Blundell Street,
London N7 9BH UK.

ISBN: 978-1-68412-329-2

Manufactured, printed, and assembled
in Shenzhen, China HH/05/18

22 21 20 19 18 1 2 3 4 5

HUMAN BODY

50

SCIENCE
EXPERIMENTS
TO MAKE AND DO

SALLY MACGILL

Silver Dolphin

GET STARTED 6

SYSTEMS OF LIFE.... 8

ZOOMING IN.......................... 8
1: HUMAN SYSTEMS............... 9
2: FLOPPY AND
   HARD POTATOES............. 10

THE SKIN............... 11

AT THE SURFACE...................... 11
3: COLD SWEAT.................... 12
4: HOW STRONG IS HAIR?...12
5: FINGERPRINT DATABASE...13
6: DUSTING FOR PRINTS...... 14

SKELETON
AND MUSCLES...... 15

BONE SUPPORT...................... 15
7: BUILDING BONES............ 16
8: BROKEN BONES............... 17
9: BEND A BONE.................. 18

JUNCTION JOINTS 19
10: BENDY BACK.................. 19
11: ROBOT HAND.................. 20

MIGHTY MUSCLES 21
12: PULLS AND PIVOTS.......... 22
13: STAND UP!....................... 23
14: FLOATING ARMS.............. 23
15: CAN YOU FEEL
    THE HEAT?...................... 24

EATING, BREATHING,
AND PUMPING
BLOOD................... 25

FEEDING TIME......................... 25
16: MASH UP! 26
17: PATH TO POOP................. 27

OXYGEN SUPPORT.................. 28
18: MODEL LUNG 29
19: LUNG CAPACITY 30

PUMPING BLOOD.................... 31
20: HEART PUMP..................... 32
21: LISTEN TO YOUR HEART... 33
22: BLOOD CIRCULATION...... 34
23: CHANGING PULSE............ 35

THE BRAIN............ 36

BRAINBOXES 36
24: THINKING CAP................. 37
25: EGG HEAD......................... 37

USE YOUR HEAD!...................... 38
26: FINDING FACES................. 38
27: MIRROR DRAWING.......... 39
28: REMEMBER THIS.............. 40
29: CATCH!............................. 41

SENSING THE WORLD.......... 42

HOW YOU FEEL...................... 42
30: HOW SENSITIVE?............. 43
31: HOT OR COLD? 44
32: RAPID REFLEX.................. 44

LOOKING AND SEEING.......... 45
33: MAKE A MODEL EYE........ 46
34: DEPTH PERCEPTION.......... 47
35: PUPIL RESPONSE.............. 47
36: ANIMATION ZOETROPE... 48
37: BLIND SPOTS.................... 49
38: SEEING 3-D...................... 50

HOW WE HEAR....................... 51
39: EAR TEST....................... 52
40: HOMEMADE HEARING
AID.................................. 53
41: MODEL EAR DRUM.......... 53
42: WHERE'S THAT SOUND?... 54

SMELLS AND TASTES.............. 55
43: SMELL DETECTIVE.............. 55
44: THE TASTE TEST.................. 56
45: SOUR TASTE....................... 57

BRAIN GAMES........................ 58
46: SPIN A COLOR.................. 58
47: MIXED MESSAGES............ 59
48: AFTER IMAGES.................. 60
49: SIXTH FINGER.................. 60
50: FAKE HAND..................... 61

GLOSSARY 62
INDEX 64

GET STARTED

Explore the human body with these 50 fun experiments. From optical illusions to robot hands, these easy-to-do projects show your body in action. Examine skin, bones, and muscles, study the brain, read how your senses work, see how your body uses nutrients, and find out how you live, thrive, and grow.

To begin, make your test tube stand by following the instructions on page 7. Then use the items in the test tube and pocket, along with everyday objects from around the house, to carry out your scientific investigations.

Equipment

Inside the test tube and box, you'll find these items. Look out for the symbol (right)—it will show you which pieces of equipment you can use from your kit.

You will nee

+ two balloons
+ plastic straw
• tape
scissors

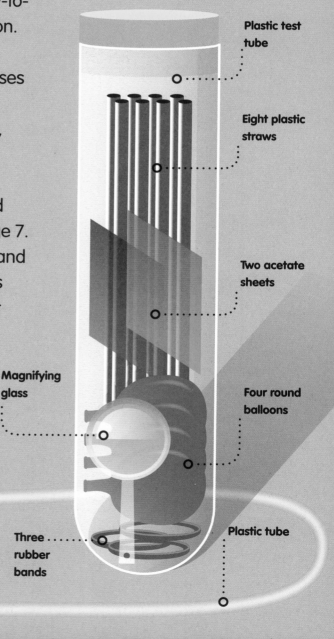

Plastic test tube

Eight plastic straws

Two acetate sheets

Four round balloons

Magnifying glass

Plastic tube

Three rubber bands

SAFETY MESSAGE

Some of the steps in these experiments may be dangerous, such as cutting items with knives. Follow the instructions carefully and ask an adult to help you when you see this symbol:

CARD KIT 1

Simply press out the parts you need

CARD KIT 2

CARD KIT 3

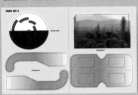

CARD KIT 4

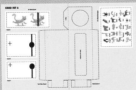

CARD KIT 5

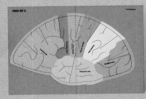

CARD KIT 6

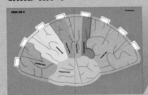

CARD KIT 7

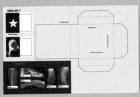

MAKE YOUR TEST TUBE STAND

1 ⚠

Tab A . . . .

Ask an adult to score and fold along all the lines on piece 1 from card kit 6. Fold it into a box shape and glue down Tab A to hold it in place. Glue down the two long tabs for a neat finish.

2 ⚠

Ask an adult to score and fold along the lines on piece 2 from card kit 7. Fold in the tabs on the small rectangles on piece 1. Push them into the slots on piece 2.

3

Open out the tabs on the small rectangles on piece 1 to hold it in place.

4

Fold in the three tabbed sides on piece 2. Glue along the tabs. Fold down the fourth side and press it onto the glued tabs.

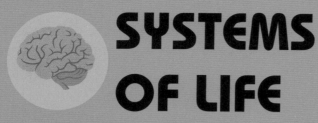

SYSTEMS OF LIFE

There's much more to your body than you can see. Lots of different body parts inside you work together so you can live, breathe, think, move, and sense what's around you. Together, these parts help your body carry out complicated processes, such as fighting germs and turning food into energy. All this activity is carefully monitored and controlled by your brain.

ZOOMING IN

You're made up of billions of tiny building blocks called **cells**. Important biological processes take place inside cells, such as making chemicals and getting energy from food. Cells also contain your **genes**, which are the coded instructions that control your characteristics, such as eye color.

Each cell has a particular job and works with other cells in one of your body's **tissues**. The blood cells look very different from the nerve cells in brain tissue because they need to perform very different tasks.

An **organ** is a group of tissues that works like a biological machine. Your heart, eyes, and brain are examples of organs. Your body's **systems** involve different organs helping each other out to perform the important jobs needed for everyday living.

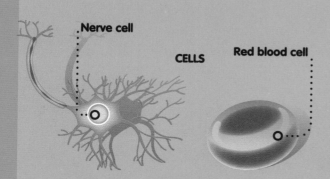

Nerve cell

CELLS

Red blood cell

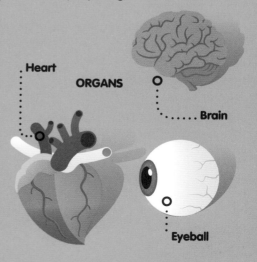

Heart

ORGANS

Brain

Eyeball

1: HUMAN SYSTEMS

You will need:
- paper
- pen

1 Look at these diagrams of some of your body's systems.

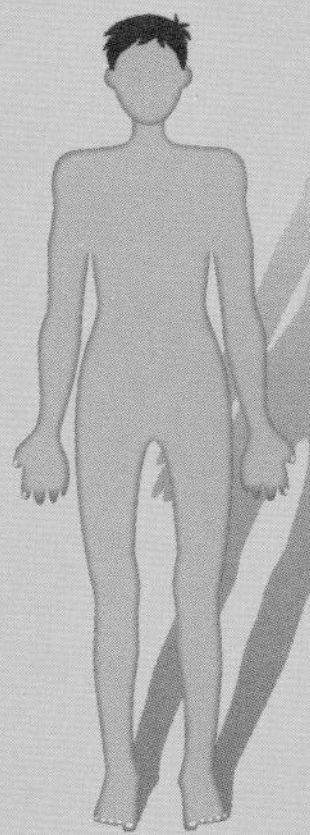

Skin, hair, and nails

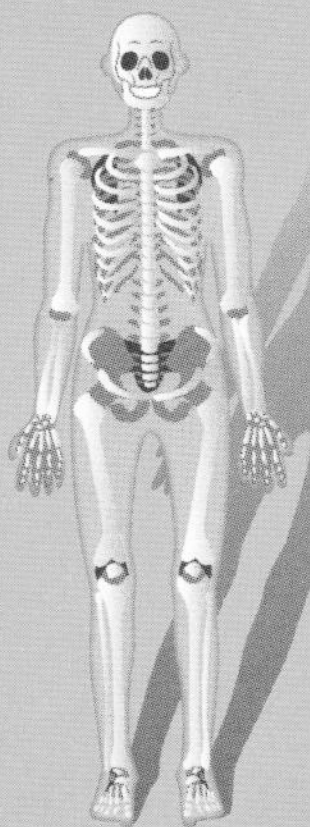

Skeletal

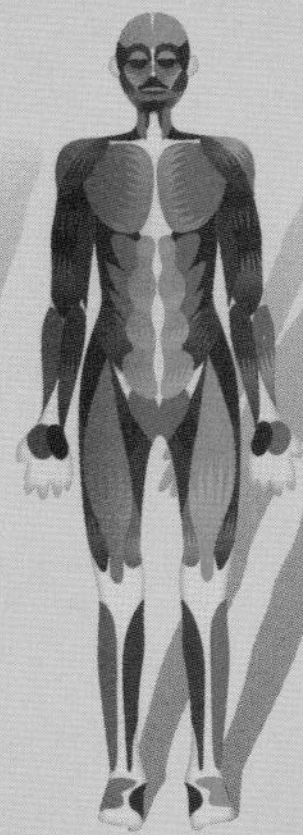

Muscular

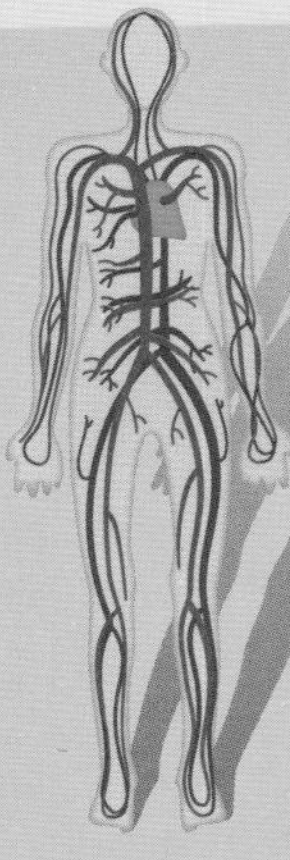

Circulatory

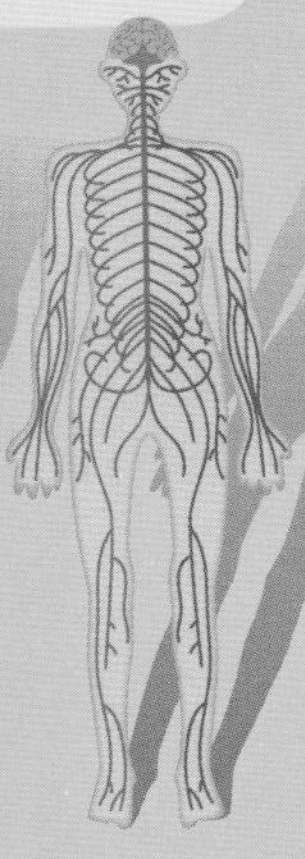

Nervous

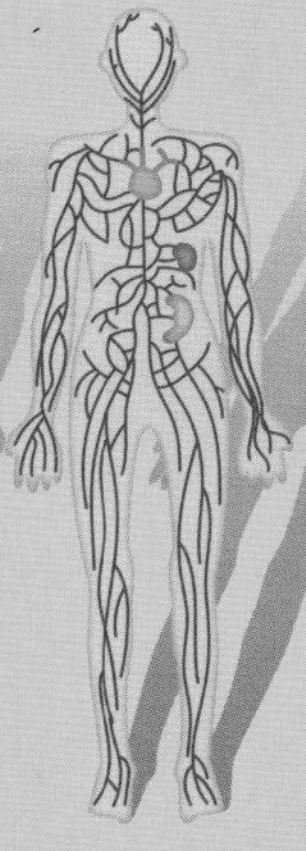

Immunity

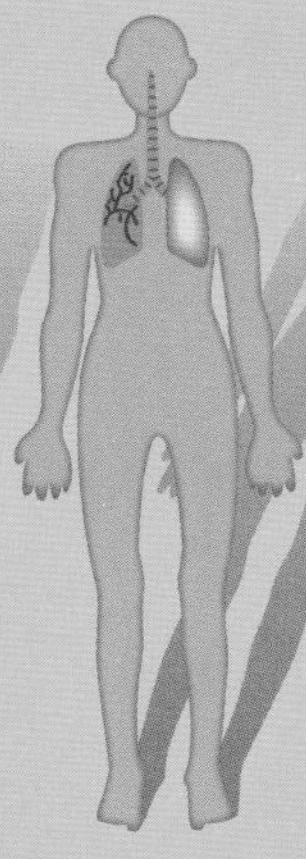

Respiratory

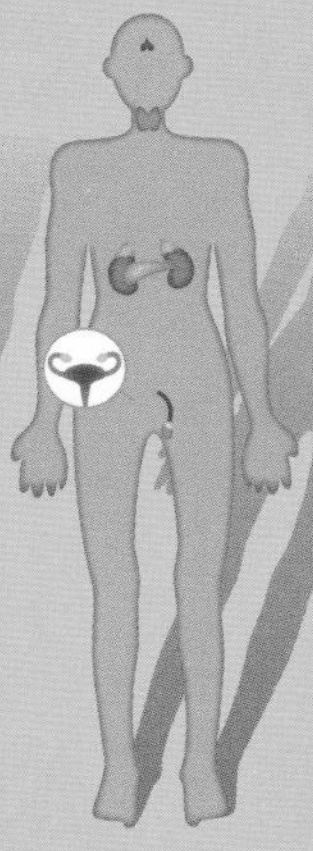

Hormones

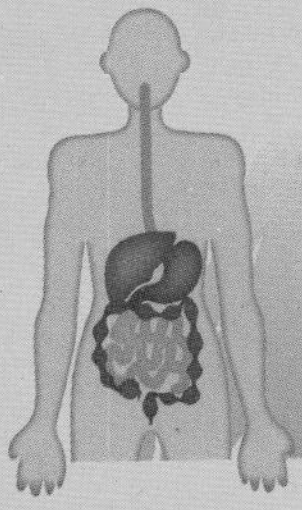

Digestive

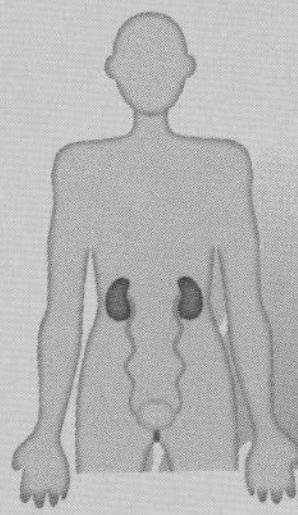

Kidneys and bladder

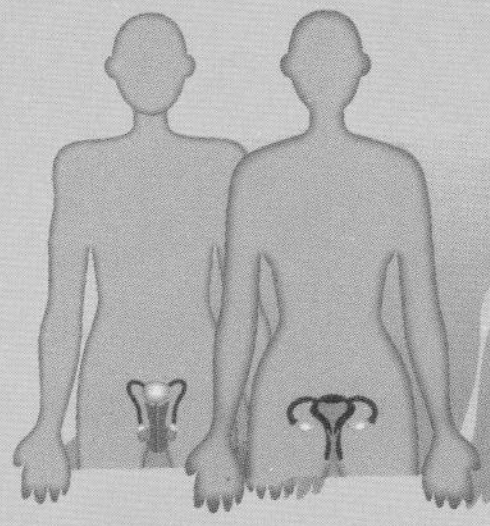

Reproductive— male and female

2 Make your own systems ID check list, with a column for some of the systems shown here, another for the main organs and structures, and a final column for functions. As you work through this book, see if you can fill in the blank columns, listing the main organs and structures and the functions of some of your body's systems.

System	Major Structures	Functions
Skeletal	Bones	Support, movement, protection, blood cell production

2: FLOPPY AND HARD POTATOES

1 Fill the bowls with lukewarm water. Add salt to one of the bowls and stir until no more will dissolve.

You will need:

- two bowls
- lukewarm water
- salt
- tablespoon
- a potato
- kitchen knife
- cutting board

2 Ask an adult to cut three slices of potato. Put a slice in each bowl and leave one slice out.

3 Leave the slices for about 30 minutes and then take them out of the water. How do they feel? Compare them to the slice that you left out. The slice that was in the very salty water should feel soft and flexible, while the slice that was in the plain water should feel quite hard and rigid.

WHAT'S HAPPENING?

The cells in the potato act like the cells in your body when they absorb water and nutrients. The outer covering of the cell will let through small particles, such as water, but block larger ones, such as salt. In the salt-water mixture, plain water moves out of the potato cells toward the liquid that has a high concentration of chemicals, leaving the potato soft and bendy. In the plain water, the concentration of chemicals is higher inside the potato cells, so water moves into them. The potato cells swell and become stiff. This process is called **osmosis**.

THE SKIN

Thin, stretchy, hairy, waterproof skin covers your whole body, holding it together and protecting it. Skin keeps water and important body fluids inside, and harmful germs outside. It allows you to feel the things you touch, and helps you keep your body at just the right temperature.

AT THE SURFACE

Skin has three layers. The outer layer is called the **epidermis** and it is tough and waterproof. It's dotted with sweat pores, and has hairs poking through it almost everywhere. Its surface is covered with dead cells.

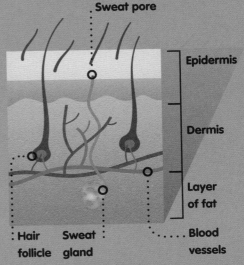

Sweat pore

Epidermis

Dermis

Layer of fat

Hair follicle   Sweat gland   Blood vessels

Underneath is the **dermis**, which is softer and more elastic. This has touch sensors, sweat glands, hair roots, and blood vessels. The hairs have glands that make oil to moisturize the skin, and there are tiny muscles that pull the hairs upright when it's cold. At the bottom is a layer of fat that stores energy, keeps you warm, and cushions your body.

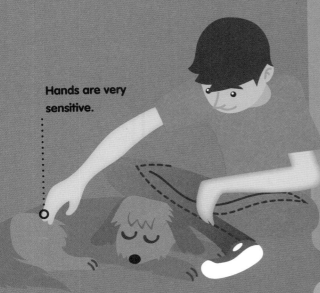

Hands are very sensitive.

Hair is constantly growing.

Although it's only about a tenth of an inch thick, the skin is the body's largest organ. It's also the fastest growing. You shed tens of thousands of skin cells every minute, and grow about ten miles of hair each year. So your body needs to work really hard to replace it all!

3: COLD SWEAT

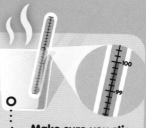

1 Ask an adult to help you mix the cold and hot water in a liquid measuring cup, and stir it. Measure the water's temperature with the thermometer and keep adding either the hot or cold water and mixing until it is about 100°F.

. . Make sure you stir the water before each reading.

You will need:

- hot and cold water from the faucet
- liquid measuring cup
- spoon to stir
- thermometer
- paper towel
- two glasses

2 Soak the paper towel in the water and wrap it around one of the glasses. Fill both glasses with the remaining water from the measuring cup.

3 After ten minutes, check the temperature of the water in the glasses. Is there a difference? See if you can tell the difference with your finger.

WHAT'S HAPPENING?

The wrapped glass should cool more quickly. The water **evaporating** from the towel takes heat from the water in the glass, cooling that water down.

4: HOW STRONG IS HAIR?

1 Wrap the hair twice around the end of the pencil and tape in place. Place the pencil on the side of a tabletop, so that the hair hangs over the edge. Tape the pencil to the table, or weigh it down with something heavy.

You will need:

- strand of hair (at least 6 inches long)
- pencil or pen
- tape
- coins
- kitchen scale

2 Using a piece of tape, stick the first coin to the other end of the hair. Carefully add more coins, adding more tape along the side of the coins. Keep adding coins until the hair snaps.

3 Remove the last coin and weigh the rest. What weight did the hair hold before it broke?

WHAT'S HAPPENING?

Hair is really strong. One strand can hold up to about 3 ounces in weight, and together a head of hair could carry two elephants!

3 oz

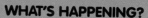

5: FINGERPRINT DATABASE

You will need:

- pencil with a soft lead (such as 2B or softer)
- paper
- tape (clear)
- + magnifying glass

1

Use the pencil to draw a solid area of gray graphite on a piece of paper, about 1 inch squared. Make sure it's well colored in.

2

Pushing down quite firmly, rub the index finger of your right hand around in the graphite until your fingertip is gray. Try to cover the finger from the tip down to the finger **joint**.

3

Stick a piece of tape on your finger. When you remove it, you should see a copy of your fingerprint clearly through the tape.

4

Mom   Dad

Create your own fingerprint database. Stick the tape sample on your database sheet and label it. Collect the fingerprints of your family and friends and add them to your database. Inspect them carefully with the magnifying glass. Are any the same?

WHAT'S HAPPENING?

Most fingerprints have a whorl, arch, or loop shape. But there's only a one in 64 billion chance that yours will be exactly the same as someone else's. They were made from pressure when your fingers developed in your mother's womb, and they are quite unique.

6: DUSTING FOR PRINTS

1 Press your index finger onto one of the plastic squares to make a fingerprint.

You will need:

- small squares of smooth rigid plastic
- fine powder (talcum powder or cornstarch)
- very soft brush (a makeup brush will work)
- tape (clear)
- colored paper
- + magnifying glass

2 Put the plastic square on a plate or piece of paper to reduce mess. Sprinkle on a small amount of the fine powder. Brush it very gently to wipe away the excess powder and you should reveal the fingerprint. If the print isn't clear, wipe the plastic clean and try it again. Rub a little moisturizer on your finger before pressing it on the plastic again.

3 Stick a piece of sticky tape over the dusted fingerprint, and press down firmly. Now gently peel it away. The print should stick to the tape. Stick this to a piece of colored paper so you can see the print. Check it against your fingerprint database. Can you recognize it as yours?

Door handles are a good source of prints. . . . . .

4 Now you can move on to dusting for prints around your house. Try dusting smooth surfaces that people touch often, such as door handles and faucets. Did you get any clear prints? Can you identify whose they are from your fingerprint database?

WHAT'S HAPPENING?

When we touch surfaces, oils on our fingers leave invisible prints of the unique pattern of ridges on our fingertips. Fine powder sticks to the oil, allowing us to see the prints.

SKELETON AND MUSCLES

Your hard, bony skeleton gives your body support and structure, so you don't just flop about. Some bones surround and protect your important organs. Others work with muscles to help you move. Your bones even make most of your blood cells—hundreds of millions of them every day!

The skull protects the brain.

The rib cage protects vital organs including the lungs and heart.

Bones come in many shapes and sizes, from tiny bones in your ears to your long leg bones. Bones meet at places called joints. Some joints, such as those in the skull, are rigid, meaning that the bones cannot move. Other joints are flexible, and the bones can move a lot.

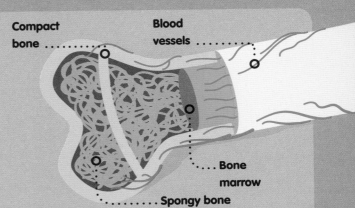

Compact bone

Blood vessels

Bone marrow

Spongy bone

BONE SUPPORT

Bone is a living tissue, which is constantly being dissolved and reshaped. When you break a bone, it can repair itself if you keep it still for a few weeks. Calcium and other minerals form a solid layer, called **compact bone**, around the outside, making bones strong. The **spongy bone** tissue underneath makes your bones lighter, so you can move them more easily. In the center is the soft **bone marrow**, where blood cells are made.

7: BUILDING BONES

1 Push out the bones from the card sheet. Look at the main image of the skeletal system and see if you can work out how the bones fit together.

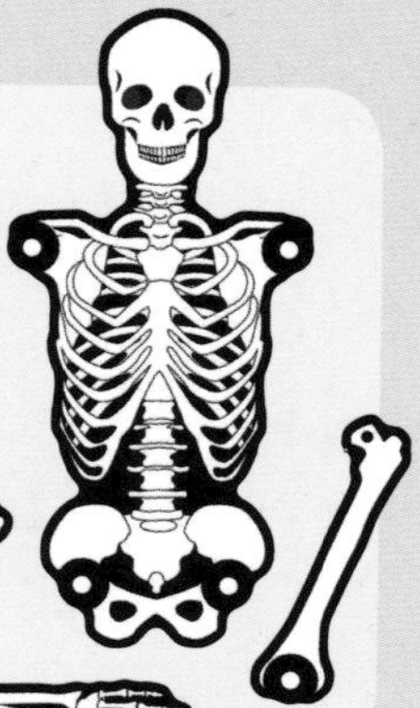

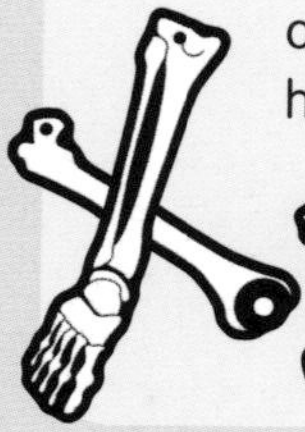

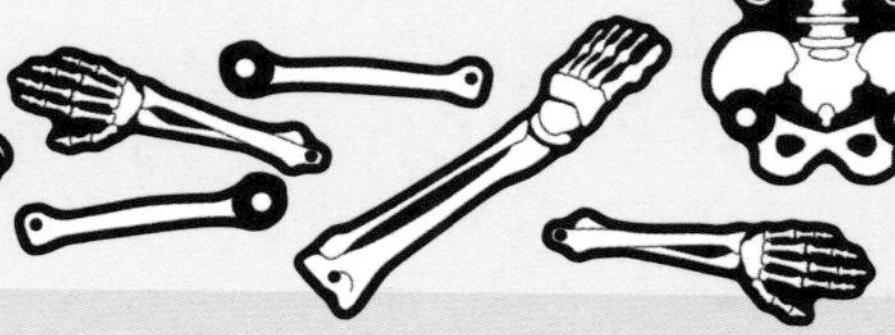

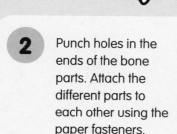

Appendicular skeleton

Axial skeleton

2 Punch holes in the ends of the bone parts. Attach the different parts to each other using the paper fasteners.

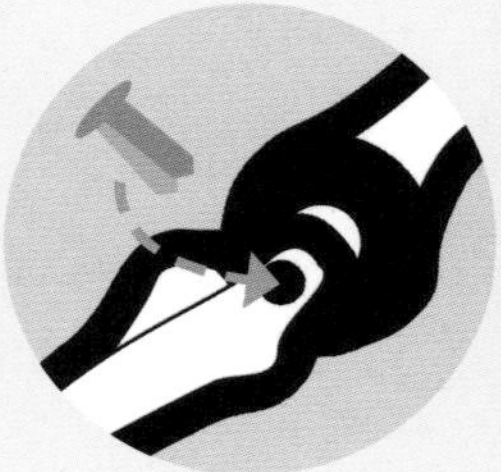

3 Using the internet, see if you can find out the names of the bones labeled A to E on the picture on the right— these are some of the largest bones in your body.

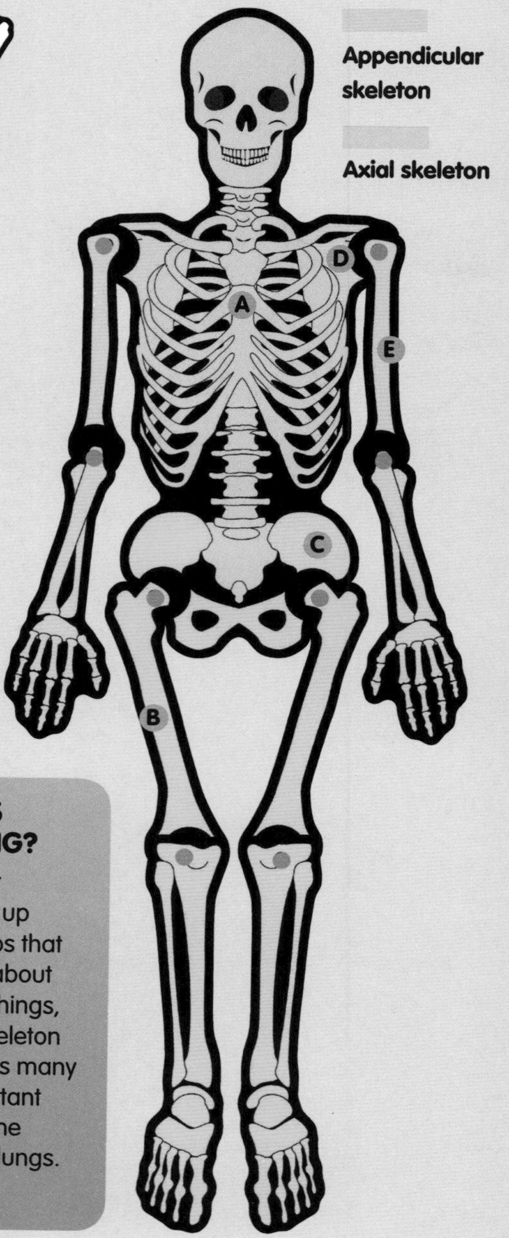

WHAT'S HAPPENING?

The appendicular skeleton is made up mainly of the limbs that help us to move about and manipulate things, while the axial skeleton holds and protects many of the most important organs, such as the brain, heart, and lungs.

4

Color in your skeleton using different colors to show the **axial skeleton** (skull, spine, and rib cage) and **appendicular skeleton** (arms, shoulders, pelvis, and legs).

Answers: A = sternum or breast bone, B = femur or thigh bone, C = ilium, D = scapula or shoulder blade, E = humerus

8: BROKEN BONES

1 Look at the **X-ray** pictures of broken bones from card kit 7. Imagine you're a doctor and someone has mixed up your patients' X-ray pictures. Can you work out which part of the body each one shows?

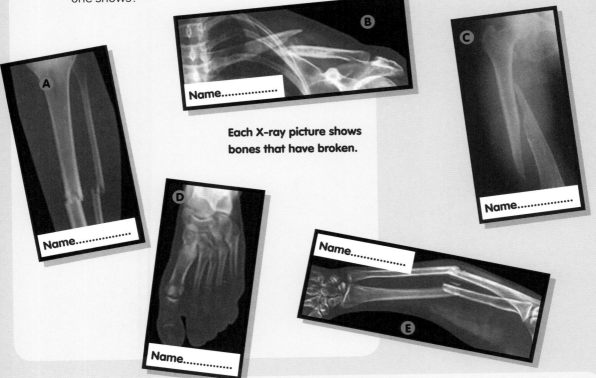

A

B

Name.................

Each X-ray picture shows bones that have broken.

C

Name.................

D

Name.................

Name.................

E

2 Now take a look at the list of your patients' injuries. Match the X-ray pictures to the injuries and write the patients' names on them so they can't get muddled up again!

1) Aisha broke her radius and ulna slipping on some ice.
2) Jack broke his clavicle wrestling.
3) Mel broke her femur in a car accident.
4) Tobias broke four of his metatarsals jumping into a swimming pool.
5) Ella broke her tibia and fibula skiing.

WHAT'S HAPPENING?

X-rays mostly pass through soft tissues, such as muscles, but they can't pass through bone. Doctors can use X-rays to make pictures of our skeletons.

Answers: A = Ella, B = Jack, C = Mel, D = Tobias, E = Aisha

9: BEND A BONE

1  Clean as much meat as you can from the bone. Try bending it. You should be able to feel that it is rigid and strong. Wash your hands before and after handling the chicken.

2 Put the bone in the test tube and pour in enough vinegar to completely cover it. Put the lid on the test tube and place it in the stand.

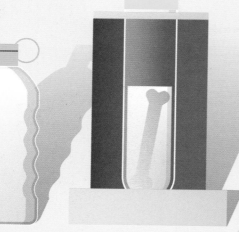

3 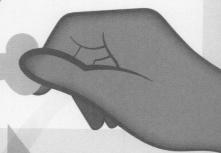 After three days, tip the contents of the test tube into a glass. Take out the bone and gently try to bend it.

4 Put the bone back in the test tube, pour the vinegar back in, replace the cap, and wait a few more days. Does more soaking time make a difference in how bendy the bone becomes?

WHAT'S HAPPENING?

Bones get their strength from a mineral called calcium carbonate in their outer coating. This slowly dissolves in vinegar, making the bones soft and flexible. Bones grow during childhood, so children need to eat lots of calcium-rich foods, such as milk, beans, and oranges.

JUNCTION JOINTS

Joints are the places where bones meet. They work in different ways, depending on how much and what type of movement is needed. Hips and shoulders have ball and socket joints, which let you swing, swivel, and twist your arms and legs quite freely. Knees and elbows have hinge joints. Like a door opening and closing, these bend in one direction. In most joints, the ends of the bones are covered in a smooth tissue called **cartilage** and surrounded by fluid. This protects the bones and helps them move more easily.

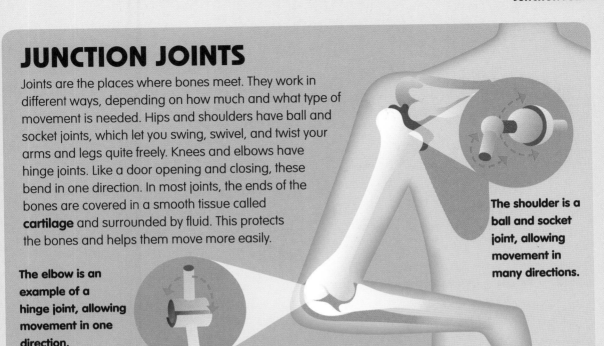

The shoulder is a ball and socket joint, allowing movement in many directions.

The elbow is an example of a hinge joint, allowing movement in one direction.

10: BENDY BACK

1 Try bending the straw gently. The material is quite rigid.

You will need:
- + plastic straw
- • pipe cleaner
- • scissors

2 Ask an adult to help you cut the straw into small pieces about half an inch long and thread these onto the pipe cleaner.

WHAT'S HAPPENING?

Your model is like your spine, a stack of small bones, called **vertebrae**, with the spinal cord running through holes in the middle. The individual joints don't move much, but together they allow you to bend your back and twist from side to side.

3 Try bending the straw again. How easily does it bend? Can it move in all directions?

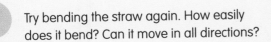

11: ROBOT HAND

1 On the sheet of thick cardboard, draw around the hand template and cut it out.

3 Stick the finger straws onto the cardboard hand using the tape, leaving the joints free of tape. Make sure the joints face upward. Ask an adult to cut short lengths of the other straw and stick these about an inch along the cardboard hand. Cut small notches in the ends of each finger and thumb using the scissors.

...... Cut here

2 Mark five of the straws with equally spaced joints as shown. Bend one of the straws over at the first joint. Ask an adult to carefully cut off slightly more than half of the bend at an angle to form a joint. Repeat with the other joints, making sure you bend them all in the same direction.

4 Push lengths of cotton thread up through each of the straws and knot them into the slits at the end of the straws to hold them in place. Wrap tape around the ends of each straw to hold the thread firmly and to strengthen the ends of the fingers and thumb.

5 Tie loops in the free ends of the thread. Tape the robot hand to your wrist and palm, and loop the thread around your own fingers and thumb. Pull with your fingers to operate the hand.

WHAT'S HAPPENING?

Most finger joints are simple hinges, which is how the straws in the robot hand work. Your knuckle joints allow your fingers to rock sideways and bend.

MIGHTY MUSCLES

Muscles are strong, elastic tissues that **contract** and relax, creating movement. They make up about half your body weight. You can control hundreds of muscles to move your bones and other body parts. You may use over 40 muscles just frowning! Other muscles keep the internal organs working without you even having to think about it. The most important and hardworking muscle is in the heart, which pumps blood around your body 24 hours a day.

Most of the muscles attached to your skeleton are long and thin. When they contract, they get shorter and fatter. This pulls the bones they are attached to, moving them. Muscles cannot push. If the joint needs to move the other way, that's another muscle's job. So many muscles, such as the large muscles on the front and back of your upper legs, work as a team.

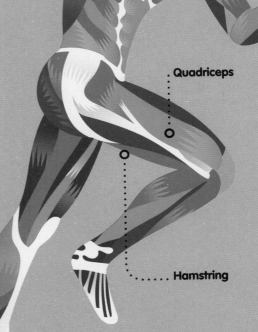

Quadriceps

Hamstring

When you run, the quadriceps muscles on the front of the thighs work to straighten the knees, while the hamstrings on the back of the thighs work to bend the knees.

When a bundle of muscle cells gets a signal to contract, chemicals inside the cells release energy for movement. This also produces lots of heat, which is why you can get hot and sweaty when you exercise.

12: PULLS AND PIVOTS

You will need:
- thick cardboard
- paper fastener
- + two rubber bands
- scissors
- pencil

1 Ask an adult to cut out two long stick shapes from some thick cardboard, about 4–5 inches long. One will be the upper arm bone (the humerus) and the other will be the two lower arm bones (the radius and ulna). Mark a dot as shown on each arm part.

Humerus

Radius and ulna

2 Ask an adult to use the pencil to punch holes where your dots are. Attach the two together using a paper fastener.

3 Cut notches on either side of the upper arm, and two more notches on the lower arm, as shown.

4 Cut the rubber bands and knot the ends. Push the knotted ends into the arm slots as shown.

Knotted ends will sit against the back of the card arms

5 Hold the arm in the middle of the humerus and pull on the rubber band on the inside of the bend, which represents contracting the **biceps**. The arm should rise up. Now pull the other rubber band—the **triceps**—and see how this pulls the arm down.

Triceps

Biceps

Hold your humerus here

WHAT'S HAPPENING?
The model shows how the biceps and triceps muscles work together as a pair. If you hold your biceps and bend your arm up, you can feel how the muscle changes shape as it contracts.

13: STAND UP!

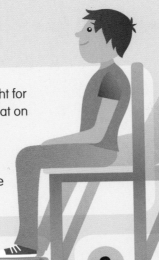

1 Find a chair that's the right height for the experiment: with your feet flat on the floor, your thighs should be horizontal. If your thighs are at an angle, try another chair or use a book to lift your feet to the right level.

You will need:
- chair
- you

WHAT'S HAPPENING?
You won't be able to stand up, however hard you try! Most of your body weight is toward the back of the chair, so you have nothing to push against to stand up. Your center of gravity needs to be over your feet for you to stand up.

2 To get into position, sit with your back straight, your feet flat on the floor, and the lower half of your legs vertical so your knees form a right angle.

3 Now fold your arms and try as hard as you can to stand up without leaning forward. Can you do it? Ask your friends and family to have a go. Can anyone stand up?

14: FLOATING ARMS

1 Stand in an open doorway, and place the backs of your hands against the insides of the door frame. Then press outward with both arms, as hard as feels comfortable, for at least 30 seconds.

2

You will need:
- you
- doorway
- clock or timer

Step away from the doorway and relax your arms. Do they start floating?

WHAT'S HAPPENING?
Your body learns that lots of effort is needed to push against the doorway. When you stop, your muscles take time to adapt to the new situation and carry on contracting. Since the doorway is no longer there, they pull your arms upward.

15: CAN YOU FEEL THE HEAT?

1 Before you start, drink a glass of water to make sure your body is well hydrated. Take your temperature and note it down. This is your resting temperature.

You will need:
- glass of drinking water
- thermometer
- timer

2 Find a step or stair and practice stepping up and down as shown below. Now find a helper to be your pacesetter, and ask them to clap twice every second. You can also use an online metronome set at 120 beats per minute. Make a step for each beat.

Right leg up → **Left leg up** → **Right leg down** → **Left leg down**

3 Step up and down at this rate for two minutes. Then stop, take your temperature again and note it down. Are you feeling hot? Has your temperature gone up?

4 Rest for two minutes, then step at the same rate for another two minutes. What's your temperature now? Has your body started sweating to lose some of the extra heat? If not, try a third set of steps.

WHAT'S HAPPENING?

As you exercised, your muscles worked hard as they contracted and relaxed, so they gave off heat and raised your body temperature by one or two degrees. When you stopped to rest, your body then lost the heat to the air, especially if you were sweating.

EATING, BREATHING, AND PUMPING BLOOD

We need energy to grow, maintain our bodies, and move around. Food supplies the fuel and chemicals we need, but everything we eat needs to be broken down first. Releasing energy from the fuel uses **oxygen**, so we also need to supply our bodies with this.

Three important systems are involved. The digestive system breaks down food and moves water and nutrients into the blood. The lungs breathe in oxygen from the air, and transfer this to the blood. The circulatory system then pumps everything in the blood around the body so that muscles and other cells can use it.

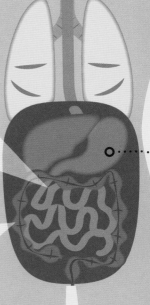

FEEDING TIME

Your teeth cut, chew, and grind food. Saliva in your mouth makes food easier to swallow, and contains an **enzyme** that starts breaking down nutrients in the food. Swallowing sends food down a tube called your esophagus (gullet) to the stomach. This is a muscly bag that churns and squashes the food, mixing it with more enzymes and acid. These break the food down more.

The next step is your small intestine, where digestive juices finish breaking down the food. Some water and most of the nutrients in the food pass through the intestine walls into your blood. The rest carries on into the large intestine. This soaks up water and minerals and stores the semisolid waste until you are ready to poop.

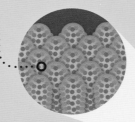

The small intestine's walls are covered with tiny fingers, so there's a huge surface area for absorbing nutrients.

Trillions of bacteria live in the large intestine, helping with the final stages of digestion.

The stomach walls make really strong acid.

25

16: MASH UP!

You will need:
- crackers
- bowl
- sealable plastic bag
- orange juice
- water
- banana

1

Put a couple of crackers into the bowl, which represents your mouth. Crush them with the back of a spoon, as you would with your teeth. You'll find a grinding movement easiest.

2 Add a few tablespoons of water—your saliva—and a large bite-sized chunk of banana. Mash it with the spoon until it looks ready to swallow.

3 Next, transfer your food to the plastic bag "stomach." Add a small amount of orange juice. This is an acid, and represents the acidic **gastric juices** in your stomach.

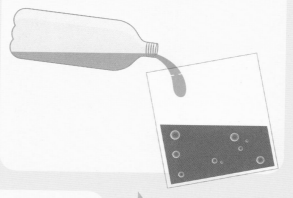

4 Seal the bag and mash the food by squeezing it between your fingers. This mimics the muscles of your stomach wall churning the food to help break it down into a sludge called **chyme**. How smooth is your chyme after a couple of minutes of stomach churning?

WHAT'S HAPPENING?
Your mashed-up food probably looks quite like chyme. However, your food spends a few hours being slowly churned in the stomach so it is really smooth. Keep your chyme to use for the next experiment.

17: PATH TO POOP

1 Ask an adult to cut one leg off the pair of pantyhose to make the small intestine. In reality, your small intestine is nearly as long as a bus!

2 Ask an adult to cut the bottom off one of the cups. Then pull the end of the pantyhose around the cup.

3 Put your intestine in the bowl. This represents your body, which needs to absorb water and nutrients. Snip one of the bottom corners off the bag of chyme and squirt the contents bit by bit into the cup. This is like the small muscle at the end of your stomach releasing chyme into your small intestine.

4

Gently push the food along to the end of the pantyhose. This is where some water and most of the nutrients in the food pass through the intestine wall into the body.

5 Ask an adult to snip the bottom of the pantyhose leg and squeeze what the body can't digest onto the kitchen towel—the large intestine. Make a hole in the bottom of the second cup. This will be the anus. Transfer the food from the towel to the cup and use the third cup to push it through the hole. You've just modeled pooping!

WHAT'S HAPPENING?

The activity models the journey of food from your stomach. As the food travels through the small and large intestines, your body absorbs everything it needs from food. A ring of muscle, called the anus, lets out unwanted material as poop.

OXYGEN SUPPORT

You need to keep breathing to stay alive. Breathing in sucks air into the body. This collects the oxygen that your body needs to make energy, and puts it into your blood. When you breathe out, you get rid of a different gas, called **carbon dioxide**, which the body makes as waste.

You breathe air in through your nose and mouth and down into your lungs. The lungs are two big, spongy organs in your chest, just under your ribs. They are linked to your nose and mouth by a tube called the trachea, or windpipe.

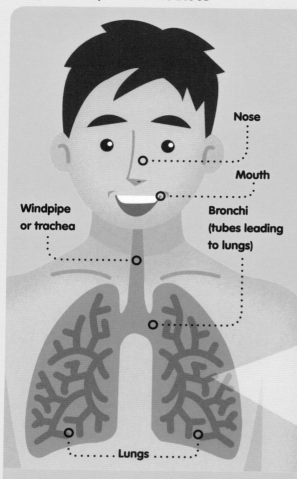

Nose

Mouth

Windpipe
or trachea

Bronchi
(tubes leading
to lungs)

Lungs

Inside the lungs, the bronchi split up into smaller and smaller tubes, called bronchioles, like a tree's branches.

At the ends of the branches, tiny blood vessels absorb the oxygen from the air.

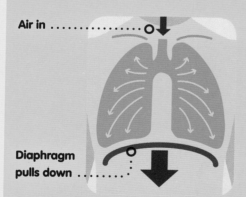

Air in

Diaphragm
pulls down

When you breathe in, muscles between your ribs lift your chest, and another muscle called the **diaphragm** contracts and pulls down. This expands the lungs, and air rushes in.

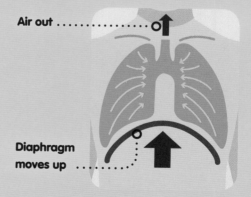

Air out

Diaphragm
moves up

When you breathe out, your muscles relax. The ribs drop down, and the diaphragm rises up. This makes the lungs smaller, pushing air out.

18: MODEL LUNG

You will need:

+ two balloons
+ plastic straw
• tape
• plastic bottle
• modeling clay
• scissors
• pencil

1

Stretch the balloons a few times to loosen them. Push the end of the straw into the nozzle of one balloon, and wrap tightly with sticky tape. Tie the nozzle of the other balloon, then ask an adult to cut it in half and throw away the top.

2

Ask an adult to cut off the top half of the plastic bottle. Stretch the cut balloon over the open end and tape it in place.

3

Make a ball of modeling clay, slightly larger than the bottle mouth, and make a hole through the middle with the pencil. Push the end of the straw through this hole, then lower the balloon end into the neck of the bottle.

4

Position the straw so the balloon hangs just below the bottle neck. Then mold the clay to form a tight seal around the straw and bottle lip.

5

Hold the bottle by the neck and pull down on the balloon at the bottom. What happens inside the bottle?

WHAT'S HAPPENING?

The balloon inside the bottle acts like one of your lungs. The cut balloon at the bottom acts like your diaphragm. When this pulls down, it increases the space around the balloon lung. This reduces air pressure around the balloon and air from outside is pushed into the balloon, making it bigger.

19: LUNG CAPACITY

1 Stick the tape all the way down one side of the bottle for your scale.

2 Measure 4 fl oz of water in the liquid measuring cup and pour into the bottle. Mark the level of the water on the tape.

3 Add water in 4 fl oz amounts until you reach the bottle's neck, marking a line on the scale for each addition. Counting from the bottom of the bottle, number every five lines to show the pint measurements.

4 Completely fill the bottle with water. Add about four inches of water to the bowl. Put your hand over the bottle mouth and place it upside down in the bowl, making sure no air gets in.

5 Push one end of the plastic tubing into the mouth of the bottle. Now take a deep breath and blow! Read your lung capacity from where the new water level is on the scale on the bottle. Ask friends to try the experiment and see who has the biggest lung capacity.

WHAT'S HAPPENING?
When you blow into the tube, the air from your lungs pushes the water out of the bottle. The largest amount of air you can breathe out is called your vital capacity.

PUMPING BLOOD

Your blood is mainly water, but each drop also contains millions of cells. Red blood cells carry oxygen. Others help blood to clot and fight **infection**. The heart pumps blood along thousands of miles of tubes called blood vessels to the cells around the body. The cells take oxygen and nutrients from the blood and get rid of carbon dioxide and other waste, which the blood then carries away.

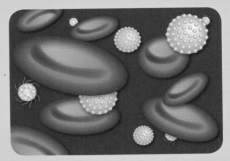

Disk-shaped red blood cells mix with spherical white blood cells and tiny platelets.

Your heart is about the size of your fist. It has four chambers and four valves that stop blood from flowing backward. Strong heart muscles squeeze the chambers, pushing blood out and around the body. When the muscles relax, the chambers get bigger and fill with blood coming back into the heart.

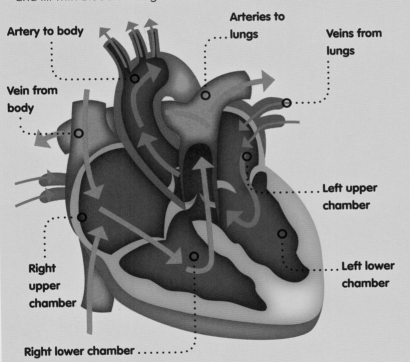

Artery to body

Arteries to lungs

Veins from lungs

Vein from body

Left upper chamber

Right upper chamber

Left lower chamber

Right lower chamber

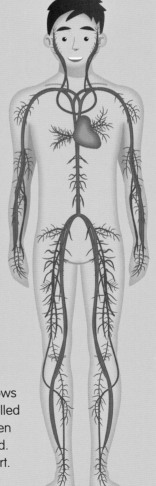

Your heart pushes blood along blood vessels called **arteries**. The blood flows through smaller and smaller arteries until it reaches the smallest tubes, called **capillaries**, which are a tenth of the thickness of a hair. This is where oxygen and nutrients move into surrounding cells, and waste moves into the blood. Wider and wider vessels called **veins** then carry the blood back to the heart. It takes just 20 seconds for blood to circulate through the whole system.

20: HEART PUMP

Tape here ⋯ ⋮ **Balloon neck**

1 Ask an adult to cut off the nozzle and the neck of the balloon. Slide the neck over the tip of one of the straws and tape it so that it is airtight. Test it by sucking the other end— it should be impossible to suck air in.

You will need:

- + balloon
- • two bendy straws
- • glass jar
- + rubber band
- • wooden skewer
- • water
- • scissors
- • tape

2 Half fill the jar with water, then stretch the body of the balloon over the jar opening. Pull it down tightly so that the top is flat and hold it in place with a rubber band.

3 Carefully poke two small holes through the balloon with the wooden skewer. They should be about an inch apart and not too close to the edges.

4 Slowly push the bottom of the straws through the holes and into the water. The balloon material should grip around the sides of the straws and stop air entering or escaping. Bend the tips of the straws out.

Press here ⋮

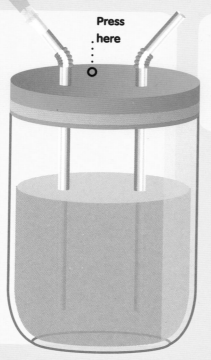

5 Place your pump in a sink. Gently push in the center of the balloon a few times. What happens to the water?

WHAT'S HAPPENING?

Pushing the balloon pumps water out through the straws. The cut end of the balloon creates a one-way valve, stopping the water going up out of the straw. One-way valves in your heart keep your blood flowing in one direction.

21: LISTEN TO YOUR HEART

You will need:

+ card cone from card kit 1
+ tape
+ plastic tube
+ balloon
• small funnel

1 Roll the card cone into a cone shape and tape it to one end of the plastic tube. This will be your ear piece.

2 Ask an adult to cut the neck off the balloon. Stretch the balloon around the large end of the funnel and tape it in place.

3 Tape the funnel to the other end of the plastic tube.

4 Now see if you can find your heartbeat. Put the earpiece on your ear, and place the balloon surface on your chest. What does it sound like? Can you hear the valves opening and closing? Try listening to other people's hearts. Do they all sound the same?

WHAT'S HAPPENING?

With each beat, you should hear a long, lower sound and a short, higher sound. These are two of your heart valves shutting at different times.

33

22: BLOOD CIRCULATION

You will need:
• a friend's arm

1 Look at the inside of your friend's forearm. If there are no blue veins running up and down, look for a suitable arm among your family and friends.

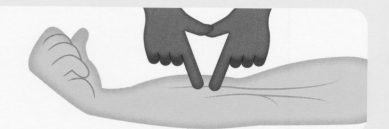

2 With your friend's arm facing upward, put two of your fingers across the vein, near to your friend's hand as shown.

3 Press down gently and slide the first finger—the one that's closer to the elbow—along the vein, keeping the second finger in place near the hand. You should see the vein emptying as you squeeze the blood out.

4 Lift the first finger. What happens to the blood in the vein? If you're not sure, repeat the process a few times and see what difference it makes if you lift the second finger first.

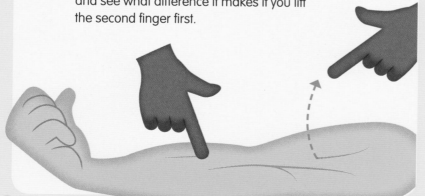

WHAT'S HAPPENING?

When you lift the first finger, the vein stays empty, but when you lift the second finger it should refill quickly. Blood flows along the vein away from the hand, toward the heart. Inside veins, tiny valves stop the blood from flowing backward.

23: CHANGING PULSE

1 First, practice taking your pulse. Put your index and middle fingers together on the wrist of your other arm, just before the joint, and with your fingertips in line with the index finger. Can you feel the blood pulsing along the artery?

You will need:
- you
- timer
- notepad
- pen

2 When you've found a reliable pulse, count the number of beats in 60 seconds. This is your heart rate in beats per minute. Once you get the hang of it, you can estimate your heart rate by counting the beats in 15 seconds and multiplying by four.

3 Take your pulse as soon as you wake up the next morning, before you've even gotten out of bed. Record the time and your pulse rate.

4 Take and record your pulse about every hour until you go to bed. Do some physically strenuous tasks, such as riding a bike, before some restful activities, such as reading. Make a note of what you were doing for each measurement.

5 Repeat the experiment on another day. Can you see any similarities with how your pulse varies on the two days? Is your pulse quick or slow when you wake up?

WHAT'S HAPPENING?

Your pulse is likely to be slowest when you wake up in the morning. When you exercise, your heart beats faster to get more oxygen to your muscles, which you need to produce energy.

THE BRAIN

Faster and more powerful than a computer, your brain is an incredibly complicated machine. A hundred billion brain cells, called neurons, send messages to control almost everything you do, even when you're asleep. Your brain is in charge of your thoughts, your personality, and how you react to the world around you. Without it, you would even forget to breathe.

BRAINBOXES

Brain scientists have divided the lumps and bumps of the cerebrum into different areas, or lobes. These have different jobs, but are linked by pathways of brain cells and constantly communicate with each other. The right half controls the left side of your body, and the left half controls the right side of your body. Scientists think the left side is more involved in math and logic, while the right deals more with abstract things, like art.

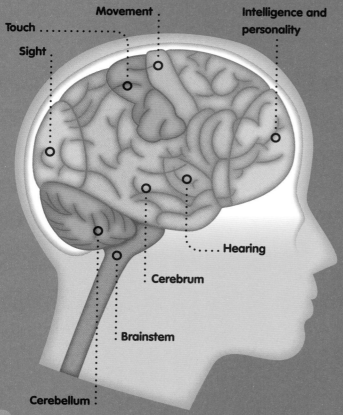

Touch

Movement

Intelligence and personality

Sight

Hearing

Cerebrum

Brainstem

Cerebellum

Brain parts

The brain has three main parts. The biggest is the cerebrum, which is where you think, sense, imagine, and control most of your muscles. The cerebellum helps you learn complicated movements such as walking and writing. The brain stem sorts messages to and from your body. It also controls your heartbeat, digestion, and other automatic actions.

24: THINKING CAP

1 Push out the two brain halves from card kit 4 and 5 and the slots in each half. Then fold in each part to the dashed line as shown, and stick in place to create a three-dimensional shape.

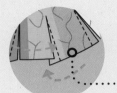

Fold at each slit so that it reaches the nearest dotted line.

WHAT'S HAPPENING?

The thinking cap shows the lobes on the cerebrum, and which area receives information from touch sensors around the body (the sensory cortex) and which area sends instructions to body parts (the motor cortex).

2 Stick both halves together using the tabs to create the whole thinking cap.

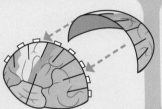

3 Place the thinking cap on your head with the frontal lobe facing the front and see the major parts, or lobes, of the cerebrum.

25: EGG HEAD

1 Place an egg in the plastic container and close the lid firmly. Think of the egg as your brain and the plastic container as your skull. Now shake it about, gently at first, and then a bit more firmly, to see how easily the egg breaks.

WHAT'S HAPPENING?

The water cushions the egg and protects it from damage. Like an egg, your brain is very delicate. But because it floats in cerebrospinal fluid, it is protected from crashing against your skull.

2 Clean the container and place the other egg inside it. This time fill the rest of the container with water before closing the lid. The water is like the clear, colorless cerebrospinal fluid that surrounds your brain. Shake the egg about again. Can you tell why the fluid is there?

USE YOUR HEAD!

Your brain cells (neurons) are joined by lots of tiny pathways. If you practice doing something, like a cartwheel, the pathways sending messages around your brain about how to do a cartwheel get stronger, making it easier for you to do great cartwheels. If you stop for a long time, it may get more difficult, as the pathways can weaken.

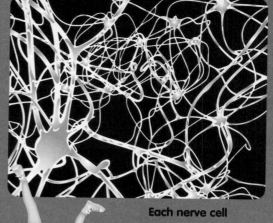

Each nerve cell in the brain is connected to thousands of other nerve cells.

Practicing a skill like cartwheeling strengthens pathways in the brain.

26: FINDING FACES

1 Look at these pictures of three objects. What do you see? Do they look like faces? Which works best, and can you say why? Try them out on friends and family and see if everyone agrees.

WHAT'S HAPPENING?

Our brains are great at recognizing faces, and we often see them in everyday objects. The eyes are usually the most important features, followed by the mouth and nose.

2 Now see if you can find objects around your house and neighborhood that look like faces. Record what you see with your camera. Look at the Internet for some inspiration—there are lots of funny examples!

27: MIRROR DRAWING

You will need:

+ star template from card kit 1
- mirror (at least 12 inches high)
- books
- paper

1

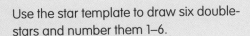

Use the star template to draw six double-stars and number them 1–6.

2 Set up a table and mirror so that, when you sit down, the mirror is vertical and about 20–30 inches in front of you.

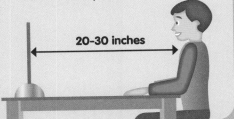

20-30 inches

3 Make two piles of books about 6 inches high and place a large book or piece of card across them to form a bridge. Position the bridge so that it will block the view of your writing hand.

Book hides your hand

4 Put drawing number 1 under the bridge and look in the mirror. Place the pencil tip anywhere between the two border lines. Then without lifting the pencil, trace all the way around the shape. Try not to go outside the lines. When you've finished, count how many times you went over a border and note it down.

5 After a ten-minute rest, repeat with the second star drawing, and then the third after another ten-minute break. Trace the final three star drawings ten minutes apart some time the following day. Did your tracing get more accurate over time, and did you remember any of what you learned after a long gap?

WHAT'S HAPPENING?

Mirror drawing is tricky, but you will get better at it the more times you repeat the experiment. Scientists use mirror learning to investigate things like the effect of poor sleep on learning these kinds of tasks.

39

28: REMEMBER THIS

You will need:
- you

1

dog, spoon, drum, swim, lemon, elephant, sock, purple

Look at the list of words in the panel above. Give yourself a minute to memorize these words. Wait five minutes and try listing them in the right order without looking at this page. Can you remember all of them?

2

Now look at the list on the panel below. Then read the paragraph that links the pictures together in a story. Try to visualize the story as much as you can when you read it. Read through the list once more, visualizing the story again. Then wait five minutes and see if you can list the items. Did you find it easier this time?

toothbrush, green, dance, flower, butterfly, camera, nose, puddle

A man with a toothbrush stuck to his lip and long, bright green hair does a dance on the head of a flower. He accidentally punches a passing butterfly. Unfortunately, the butterfly had a really expensive camera hooked on its nose, which fell to the ground and bounced into a huge puddle.

3

Now see if you can make up a story for the list below. Try to come up with really strong visual images. The more silly and surprising the pictures you can make in your head, the easier it will be to memorize the list.

ladder, square, whale, jewel, holiday, cave, ice cube, honey

4

Try to recite the three lists again the next day, with just the first word of each as prompts. Can you remember any full lists? Which do you remember best?

WHAT'S HAPPENING?

You'll probably find it easier to remember the list of words by using them in a story. You'll also find it easier to remember the words using a story that you can visualize the best.

29: CATCH!

You will need:
- ruler
- notepad
- pen or pencil

1 Hold your arm out straight in front of you, with your fingers on top of each other and thumb slightly off to the side. Ask a helper to hold the ruler vertically, with the base between your thumb and index finger.

2 Ask the helper to drop the ruler without warning you. When you notice it drop, try to catch it as quickly as you can.

3 Write down the measurement from the top of your thumb. Look at the conversion table here and see how quickly you reacted.

DISTANCE	TIME
2 in	0.10 sec (100 ms)
4 in	0.14 sec (140 ms)
6 in	0.17 sec (170 ms)
8 in	0.20 sec (200 ms)

4 Try again and see if you can beat your time. Then switch roles and test your helper's reaction time.

WHAT'S HAPPENING?

Messages in the brain can travel up to 250 miles per hour. This means that it probably only takes about 0.15 seconds for your brain to see the ruler falling and tell your hand to catch it. If your brain is distracted with a tricky task, such as doing math, it will be much slower.

SENSING THE WORLD

Your body contains billions of tiny sensors. They send signals to your brain, telling it what is going on in your body and the world around you. There are five main senses: sight, hearing, taste, touch, and smell. Other sensors tell your brain how your body is performing, where its various parts are, and even which way is up!

Combining senses

Eating a meal can involve many of your senses. Your eyes see the food you are about to eat. Your nose smells the food. Touch sensors in and around your mouth feel the satisfying crunch as you bite into the food. And, of course, taste sensors on your tongue tell you what flavor the food is.

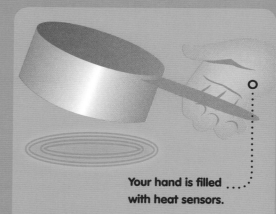

Your hand is filled with heat sensors.

Your sense of taste is enhanced by other senses.

HOW YOU FEEL

Sensors just under the surface of your skin detect pressure, heat, cold, pain, and vibration. They are concentrated in the parts of your body that really need them, and they can help to protect you from damage from stings, burns, and sharp objects.

30: HOW SENSITIVE?

1 Open a paper clip out, then bend it over to make a U shape. Show your volunteer the paper clip and tell them you will touch them with either one or two points on different parts of their body. Ask them to keep their eyes closed throughout the experiment.

2 Use the ruler to set the gap between the points on the first paper clip to 2 inches. Then touch the points in the middle of your volunteer's palm, putting equal pressure on both. Note down whether they can feel one or two points.

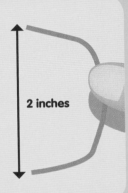

2 inches

3 Now open out the other paper clips to the following widths: 1½ inches, 1 inch, ½ inch, ¼ inch, and ends touching. Test your volunteer's palm again, using the paper clips in a random order. You'll probably find they can easily tell two points 1 inch apart, but are not confident when the points are ½ inch apart, and can only feel the paper clips with a smaller gap as a single point.

4 Now move on to the other parts of the body marked above. You can miss out smaller distances once your volunteer says they only feel one point. Put the body areas in order of skin sensitivity.

WHAT'S HAPPENING?

If just one skin sensor is stimulated by the two points, the brain registers them as one point. More sensitive parts of your body will be able to detect smaller gaps.

31: HOT OR COLD?

2

Wrap one hand around the cold water glass, and the other around the hot. Make sure your palms are touching the glasses. Hold the glasses for at least 60 seconds.

3

Put the glasses down and quickly grasp the room temperature glass with both hands. How hot does it feel to you?

You will need:

- three glasses
- water
- timer

1 Fill one glass with iced water, one glass with water from the hot faucet, and one with water at room temperature.

WHAT'S HAPPENING?

The hand that held the hot water will feel the glass as much colder than the one that held iced water. Rather than measuring temperature, your skin is sensitive to temperature changes.

32: RAPID REFLEX

You will need:

- volunteer
- chair

2

Using the side of your hand, gently tap their leg just below the knee. If the leg doesn't move, try it again in a slightly different place. When you tap the right place, the leg should jerk up.

WHAT'S HAPPENING?

This knee jerk is a type of reflex action. These do not involve instructions from the brain and pass only through the spinal cord.

1

Find a volunteer to sit on a chair and cross their legs so the top one can swing freely from the knee. Ask them to relax as much as they can.

Tap here

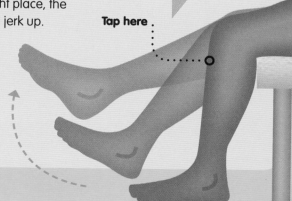

LOOKING AND SEEING

Your eyes are in a perfect position to sense light bouncing off objects in front of you, giving you a pin-sharp picture of the world.

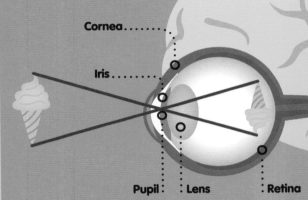

Cornea

Iris

Pupil

Lens

Retina

Visual cortex

Rays of light pass through the cornea at the front of each eyeball and enter the eye through a hole called the pupil. The size of this hole changes in response to light levels— it gets bigger when it is dim so you can see better, and smaller when there is a lot of light to stop you from getting dazzled. The lens helps to focus light on the retina at the back of the eye. Muscles change the shape of the lens to help it focus on objects at different distances.

The retina at the back of the eye is covered with millions of light-sensitive cells. These convert the image into nerve signals that are sent along the optic nerve to a region at the back of the brain called the visual cortex. Here, the signals are interpreted by the brain as visual images.

3-D vision

Each eye sees a slightly different view of the world. Your brain puts these different pictures together to produce a three-dimensional image. This allows you to judge how far away objects are.

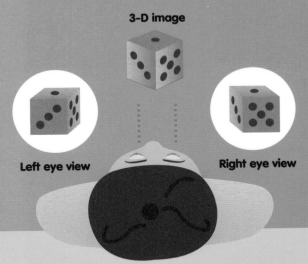

3-D image

Left eye view

Right eye view

33: MAKE A MODEL EYE

1 Put a ruler on a table in front of you with a bright window behind you several feet away. Hold the magnifying glass at 0 inches on the ruler. Then slowly slide a small piece of white paper backward and forward along the ruler until a sharp image of the scene in the window appears on the paper.

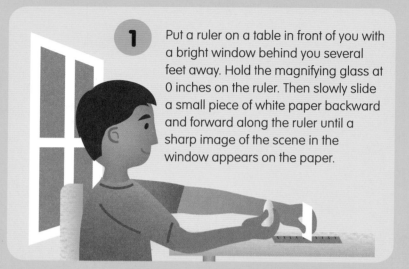

You will need:
- ruler
- **+ magnifying glass**
- piece of white paper
- black paper
- tracing paper
- tape

2 Write down where the paper is on the ruler. This is the focal length of the magnifying glass.

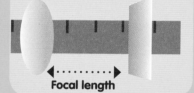

Focal length

3 Cut a strip of black paper with a width that matches the focal length. Roll the paper to form a tube with a length equal to the focal length and a diameter the same size as the magnifying glass.

4 Tape the magnifying glass to one end of the tube. This is the lens at the front of your eye. Then tape a piece of tracing paper to the other end to make a retina—the light-sensitive area where the image is formed.

5 Go outside and test your eye. Point it at a bright scene, and you should see an image of the scene appear on the paper. But it will be upside-down!

WHAT'S HAPPENING?
The lens should focus an upside-down image on the paper. The image on your retina is also upside-down, but your brain flips it over so that you see the world the right way up.

34: DEPTH PERCEPTION

You will need:
• two pencils

1 Hold the two pencils at arm's length in front of you with the tips facing each other and about 12 inches apart. Slowly move the tips together so they touch. Can you do this quite easily?

2 Close one eye and try it again. Is it trickier?

WHAT'S HAPPENING?

With two eyes, you can compare images at slightly different angles to work out exactly how far away each pencil is. With just one eye, you can't tell which is further away, so the task is trickier.

35: PUPIL RESPONSE

1 Close the curtains or dim the lights so the room is quite dark. Ask a volunteer to stand in the darkened room for a few minutes.

You will need:
• volunteer

2 Once they've gotten used to the dim light, take a look at their eyes. The pupil—the black dot in the center—should be quite large.

3 Keep looking at the eyes while you turn the lights on. Do the pupils change size?

WHAT'S HAPPENING?

While the room was dark, the pupils expanded to take in as much light as possible. As soon as the lights were switched on, a reflex response caused the pupils to rapidly contract to protect the retina.

36: ANIMATION ZOETROPE

1 Fold the ends of the drum part of the zoetrope template round and stick them in place with tape. Wrap the top part of the zoetrope into a cylinder and push it inside the drum.

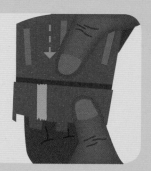

2 Holding the drum and top parts together, attach them to the disk base by pushing the tabs on the drum through the slits in the disk.

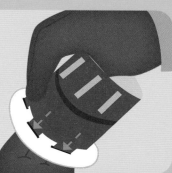

3

Wrap the animation strip into a cylinder and push it inside the drum, making sure that the slits are above the animation strip.

4

Push a pencil through the hole in the base, then use it to spin the zoetrope. Look through the slits while it's spinning. It should look like the pictures are moving!

5 Try drawing your own animation strip on the reverse side of the strip from the card kit.

WHAT'S HAPPENING?
Your brain sees the changing images as continuous movement, filling in the gaps between images. The same thing happens when we watch a movie, which is made up of a rapidly changing series of still images.

37: BLIND SPOTS

1

Hold card 1 at arm's length. Close your left eye and use your right eye to look at the cross on the left.

You will need:
+ blind spot
cards from
card kit 6

2

Slowly bring the card toward you. Keep focusing on the cross, but note whether you can still see the spot. What happens as the card approaches your face? Does the spot disappear for a short while?

3

Try the same thing with card 2. The spot should disappear at the same distance from your eyes. But what can you see in its place? Is the spot replaced with a line?

4

Now look at the two cats on card 3. They are both the same size, but what happens if you look at the picture when the wall is in your blind spot? Does the cat behind the wall look the right length?

WHAT'S HAPPENING?

There are no light sensors where the optic nerve joins the retina, so you can't see images in this area. This is your blind spot. Your brain fills in the blank areas using information from around the blind spot—it should even shrink the cat!

49

38: SEEING 3-D

1 Push out the pieces for your 3-D glasses.

You will need:

+ glasses template from card kit 3
+ red and blue pieces of acetate
• tape
+ anaglyph image from card kit 3

2 Stick the blue cellophane over the hole for your right eye and the red cellophane over the hole for your left eye.

3

Stick the arms of your 3-D glasses to the sides as shown.
Then fold over the top half of the eyepieces and stick it in place.

4

Fold back the arms and put your glasses on, making sure the blue cellophane is over your right eye and the red cellophane is over your left eye. Then look at the anaglyph image from the card kit—does it look 3-D?

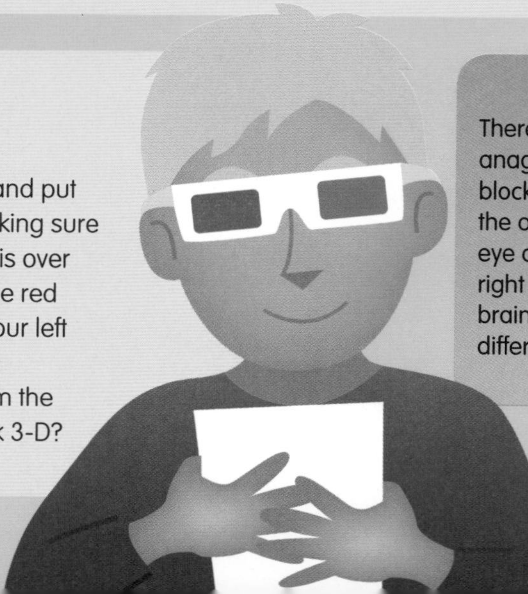

WHAT'S HAPPENING?

There are two images on the anaglyph. Each lens in your glasses blocks one colored image and lets the other one through, so the left eye only sees one image, and the right eye only sees the other. Your brain interprets the two slightly different images as one 3-D image.

HOW WE HEAR

The ears on either side of your head are two flappy funnels that collect sounds and form the outer parts of the complicated system that allows you to hear.

Sounds are made up of vibrations. As these vibrations move through the air, they are collected and funneled by your outer ears into a tube called your ear canal, which leads into your head. At the end of the ear canal is a tiny membrane called the eardrum. The vibrations in the air cause the eardrum to vibrate.

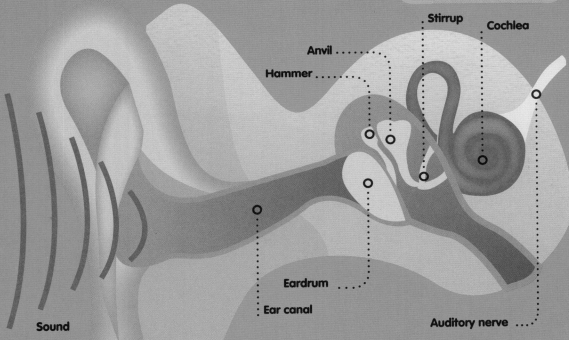

Stirrup

Cochlea

Anvil . . . .

Hammer . . . .

Eardrum . . . .

Ear canal

Sound

Auditory nerve . . . .

On the other side, the eardrum is attached to three tiny bones called the ossicles (the hammer, anvil, and stirrup). The ossicles transmit and amplify (make louder) the vibrations, and pass them on to a liquid inside a coiled structure called the cochlea.

As the vibrations move through the liquid inside the cochlea, they are picked up by tiny sensitive hairs. The hairs turn the vibrations into nerve signals, which are sent along the auditory nerve to a part of the brain called the auditory cortex. Here, the brain interprets the nerve signals and hears the sound.

39: EAR TEST

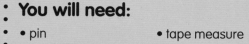
1 Ask your volunteer to stand close to a table, with their back to it, and raise a hand if they can hear the sound of a pin hitting the table.

2 Drop a pin on to the table from a height of 6 inches. Use the ruler to measure the distance.

3 If your volunteer raises their hand, ask them to take one step away from the table, then repeat the test. Do this until they can no longer hear the pin drop. Measure the distance they are from the table.

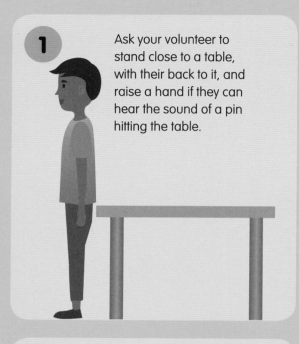

4 Now test other people, and ask someone to test you. Who has the best hearing? Does their age make a difference? Try dropping other objects, such as an eraser. How does this affect the results?

WHAT'S HAPPENING?
As you move farther away from the sound, the vibrations reaching the ear become smaller so are harder to hear. People gradually find it harder to hear quiet and high-pitched sounds as they get older.

40: HOMEMADE HEARING AID

You will need:

- pin
- ruler
- tape measure
- volunteer
- newspaper or thin cardstock
- tape

1 Carry out an ear test on a volunteer, as described in the last experiment.

2

Roll a couple of sheets of newspaper to form a wide cone shape, and tape it together. Ask an adult to trim the small end to make a hole about half an inch across.

3 Ask your volunteer to hold the cone against one of their ears and test their hearing again. The cone will need to point at the table, so they should close their eyes. Has their hearing improved?

WHAT'S HAPPENING?

The end of the cone is bigger than your ear, so it collects more sound waves. This allows you to hear quiet sounds more clearly.

41: MODEL EAR DRUM

You will need:

- music player and headphones
- plastic cup
- scissors
- plastic wrap
- rubber band
- fine salt

1 Ask an adult to cut the top 3 inches off the plastic cup. Stretch some plastic wrap over the top of the cup and secure with a rubber band.

2

Sprinkle some salt onto the surface.

3 With your headphones playing some loud music, hold them close to the surface of the plastic. Does anything happen to the salt? Try different types of music and see which works best.

WHAT'S HAPPENING?

The speaker produces sound waves, which makes the plastic vibrate and the salt jump about.

42: WHERE'S THAT SOUND?

You will need:

- volunteer
- blindfold
- string 100 feet long
- three tent pegs
- protractor
- pen
- notebook

1 Find a large open area for your experiment. Ask a volunteer to stand in a place with about 50 feet of free space in front and to the sides of them.

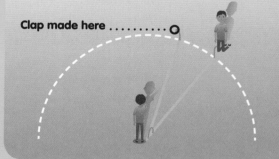

50 feet

50 feet   50 feet

2 Tie a tent peg to each end of the string, then another in the middle of it. Peg the middle of the string down just in front of your volunteer. Put a blindfold on them, tell them to face forward and when they hear you clap point in the direction they think the sound came from.

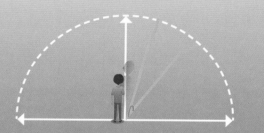

3 Pull one end of the string out tight and peg it into in the ground, then clap your hands three times. Move around in a semicircle to where your volunteer is pointing and put the other peg in the ground (unless they point straight at you!).

Clap made here . . . . O

4 Use the protractor to measure the angle the clap was made from and the angle between the two strings, and record this data in a table. Then repeat the process, mixing up the directions. Do your results give you an indication of which directions we can most accurately identify sound from?

WHAT'S HAPPENING?

If a sound is coming from the side, one ear hears it just before the other ear. Our brains use this difference to work out where the sound is coming from. This is much more difficult if the sound is in front of us, as it reaches both ears at the same time.

SMELLS AND TASTES

Sniffing the air draws air particles into the space inside your nose called the nasal cavity. Scent particles in the air are trapped by tiny hairs called cilia in the roof of the nasal cavity. Special receptor cells send signals to the brain.

There are thousands of taste buds on the surface of your tongue and on the back of your mouth. They have receptor cells that are sensitive to five different flavors— sweet, sour, bitter, salty, and umami (savory).

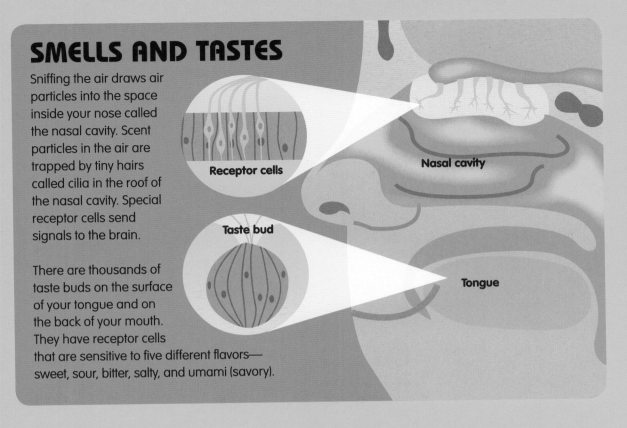

Receptor cells

Nasal cavity

Taste bud

Tongue

43: SMELL DETECTIVE

1 Gather some clothes belonging to friends and family, ones they've worn recently and that have not been laundered.

You will need:
- volunteer
- "dirty" clothes
- blindfold

2 Put on a blindfold and ask a helper to hold the items in front of your nose in a random order.

3 Can you guess from the smell whose clothing it is? Try smelling different areas of the items. Does this make a difference?

WHAT'S HAPPENING?

We all have a unique smell, which rubs off on our clothes. The smell comes from chemicals called pheromones, which are produced by our bodies.

44: THE TASTE TEST

You will need:

- assortment of fruit and vegetables
- sheet of paper
- blindfold
- volunteer
- knife
- spoon
- pen

2 Find a volunteer who hasn't seen the food you want them to taste. Put a blindfold over their eyes and ask them to hold their nose closed. Use a spoon to feed them a piece of food and ask them to identify what it is. Write their answer on your record sheet.

1 Choose three fruits and three vegetables that have a similar texture and ask an adult to cut them into small chunks. Remove any skin or seeds that could help identify what they are. List the names of the foods on the paper.

3 Give your taster two samples of each food. Make the order as random as possible and record their responses as you go along.

4 Repeat the taste test with your taster not holding their nose, so they can smell as well as taste what they are eating. Are some foods easier to identify than others?

WHAT'S HAPPENING?

When we taste food, we use information from both our taste buds and our noses. If we are not able to smell the food, we find it hard to identify it. This is why food can taste bland when we have a cold and our noses are blocked.

45: SOUR TASTE

1 Using the test tube as a measure, add a tube-full of water to each of the three cups. Label them A, B, and C.

A   B   C

2 Add the juice of half a lemon to cup A, the juice of a whole lemon to cup B, and the juice of one and a half lemons to cup C. If you're using lemon juice, add 1½ tablespoons to cup A, 3 tablespoons to B, and 4½ tablespoons to C.

A   B   C

3 Now add 2 teaspoons of sugar to A, 1½ teaspoons of sugar to B and just ½ a teaspoon of sugar to C. Stir well to make sure all the sugar has dissolved.

A   B   C

4 Pour a small amount of each mixture into the three testing cups. One by one, ask each family member to taste the three cups and say which one they like best. Note down the results. Do you notice a relationship between people's age and their preferences?

WHAT'S HAPPENING?

You may find that children are likely to prefer the liquid in cups B and C, while adults will probably prefer the liquid in cups A and B. Scientists are still unsure why this age difference in taste occurs.

BRAIN GAMES

Your body collects information from around you and sends it to your brain, where it is interpreted to make sense of the world. However, some combinations of signals (sounds, images, and feelings) can trick the brain, making it believe that something is there when it really isn't.

These are called illusions, and you can have great fun making and testing some of your own.

Can you see a triangle in the center of this image? Is it really there?

46: SPIN A COLOR

You will need:
- **+ card circle from card kit 3**
- • pencil
- • tape or glue

1

⚠️

Remove the disk and ask an adult to make a hole in the center using the pencil. Push the pencil through the hole and use tape or glue to stick the underside of the disk to the pencil.

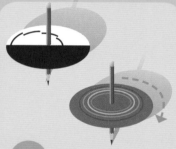

2

Experiment with spinning the disk between your palms at different speeds, while looking at the rings. Do they join up to make complete circles? Are they all black or do some appear colored? Adjust the spinning speed until you see color.

3

Try spinning in the opposite direction. What happens to the colors?

WHAT'S HAPPENING?

Spinning the disk quite slowly makes different colored rings appear, with red and blue on the inside or outside. Spinning in the opposite direction reverses the order of the colors. Scientists don't yet fully understand why this happens, but it may be because we see some colors slightly quicker than others.

47: MIXED MESSAGES

You will need:

+ card sheet with animals from card kit 6
• timer
• colored pens

1

Take out the animals sheet and look at the side with the correct names on it. Time yourself to see how quickly you can name each of the animal pictures.

2

Now turn the sheet over to where the animals are incorrectly named and try it again. Make sure you name the animal picture, not the animal name written below.

3

Now let's make a similar experiment to test your friends and family. Draw a 5 by 5 grid on a piece of paper, so you have 25 rectangles. In each rectangle, write the name of a color using a pen of that color. So write the word "red" using a red pen, the word "blue" using a blue pen, and so on. Use five or six colors and try to spread them evenly around the grid.

4

Draw another grid on a second piece of paper. Use the same colors and words, but this time write the color name using a different colored pen. For instance, you could write the word "red" using a blue pen. Time how long it takes your friends to list the colors in both test cards.

WHAT'S HAPPENING?

It should be more difficult to identify the animals and colors if the words don't match. Since you learned to read, your brain is strongly influenced by written words, even if you are trying to ignore them.

48: AFTER IMAGES

1

Stare at the dot in the center of the picture for 20–30 seconds, fixing your gaze. Then look at the white area. Can you see a black star?

2

Try it with the negative photo image. What can you see this time?

You will need:

+ after image pictures from card kit 7

WHAT'S HAPPENING?

On white, you should see a negative of the image you stared at. This is called an after image. Light receptors in your eyes become less sensitive when you stare at something, and take time to readjust back to normal. The eyes have different receptors for different colors—color after images are made up of images using the receptors that are still working normally.

49: SIXTH FINGER

You will need:
• mirror   • volunteer

1 Sit opposite a volunteer at a table. Ask them to put their hands flat on the table, about 12 inches apart. Place the mirror between their hands so it hides one hand, but allows them to see the other hand in the mirror.

2 Stroke your volunteer's left and right thumbs at the same time, from knuckle to tip, then along the length of each of their left and right fingers. Count "1, 2, 3, 4, 5", with one number for each digit.

3 Start stroking again from the thumb. But this time, when you reach 5, stroke along the inside of the hidden little finger while stroking along the top of the visible little finger. Then count 6, and stroke along the outside of the hidden little finger.

WHAT'S HAPPENING?

This experiment uses sight and touch to trick the brain into thinking the hand has an extra finger.

Mirror

Hidden hand

Visible hand

50: FAKE HAND

You will need:
- rubber glove
- cotton wool
- volunteer
- large book to use as a screen
- towel
- two paintbrushes

1 Stuff a right-hand rubber glove with cotton wool so it looks like there's a real hand inside.

2 Make a vertical screen about 12 inches high and 8 inches wide. This can just be a large book.

3 Ask a volunteer to sit in the chair and put their right hand on the table, palm down, to one side. Place the fake hand palm down in front of them. Put the screen upright between their right hand and the fake hand and drape the towel over the wrists of both. Make sure they can't see their real hand.

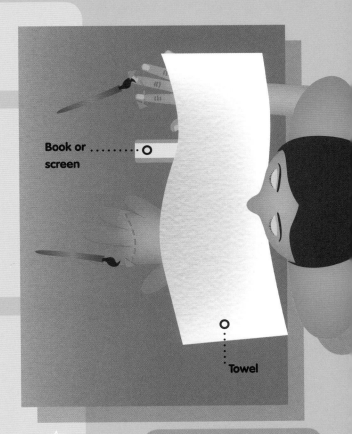

Book or .... O
screen

O
⋮
Towel

4 Use the two paintbrushes to gently stroke the fingers on your volunteer's right hand, while stroking the same fingers on the fake hand at the same time. Make sure they watch the fake hand while you do this.

5 After about a minute of stroking, slam your hand down on the fake hand. How do they react?

WHAT'S HAPPENING?

Your volunteer's brain was tricked into believing that the fake hand was their hand. They are likely to have pulled away their own right hand as a reflex reaction when you hit the fake hand.

GLOSSARY

APPENDICULAR SKELETON
The part of your skeleton that is made up of your arms, shoulders, pelvis, and legs.

ARTERIES
Blood vessels that carry blood away from the heart. They usually have thick, muscular walls because they carry blood that is under high pressure.

AXIAL SKELETON
The part of your skeleton that is made up of your skull, spine, and rib cage.

BACTERIA
Very small living things that are made up of a single cell. While some can be harmful to you, the human intestine contains trillions of friendly bacteria that help us to digest food.

BICEPS
The muscles at the front of the upper arm. These pull on the lower arm to bend the arm at the elbow.

BONE MARROW
A jellylike substance that is found inside bones. It is where red blood cells are made.

CAPILLARIES
The tiny blood vessels that link arteries and veins. Many have walls that are only a cell thick so that nutrients and oxygen can pass from the blood and into the body's cells, while waste products move the other way.

CARBON DIOXIDE
An odorless and colorless gas that is a waste product made by cells when they produce energy. It is carried from the body's cells by the blood to the lungs, where it is breathed out.

CARTILAGE
A flexible tissue that is found in joints between bones and also forms the shape of your nose and ears.

CELLS
The tiny building blocks of living things.

CHYME
The thick, gunky fluid that is produced when your stomach mashes up the food you've swallowed with the gastric juices it has produced.

COMPACT BONE
A type of bone that is formed of densely packed bone tissue. It makes up about 80 percent of the human skeleton and, in longer bones, it forms a shell around the spongy bone tissue.

CONTRACT
To get smaller.

DERMIS
The layer of skin just below the epidermis. It contains the hair follicles, sweat glands, and blood vessels, as well as the touch sensors.

DIAPHRAGM
A dome-shaped sheet of muscle tissue that sits beneath your lungs. The diaphragm contracts and flattens to make the lungs larger when we breathe in air.

ENZYME
A special type of chemical that speeds up the rate of chemical reactions. Your body produces digestive enzymes to break food up into simpler parts so that they can be absorbed and used to produce energy or make new body parts.

EPIDERMIS
The top layer of skin. It provides a hard-wearing protective surface that is covered by toughened, dead skin cells. These are continually being shed and then replaced by other skin cells from beneath.

EVAPORATING
When a liquid turns into a gas.

GASTRIC JUICES
The mixture of acid and digestive enzymes that are produced by the stomach and mixed with any swallowed food.

GENES
The parts of a living cell that control how it looks and behaves. Genes are made up of long sequences of a chemical known as deoxyribonucleic acid (DNA).

HAMSTRING
The muscles at the back of the upper legs, they pull on the lower leg to bend the knee.

INFECTION
A disease caused by germs or bacteria.

JOINTS
The points where two or more bones meet. Joints can be rigid, such as the fused joints between the skull bones, or flexible, such as the joints in your arms and legs.

ORGAN
A body part that is formed from a collection of tissues and has a specific role. Examples include your heart, brain, and lungs.

OSMOSIS
The movement of a liquid from an area of low concentration to an area of high concentration through a membrane with tiny holes, such as the wall of a cell.

OXYGEN
An odorless and colorless gas that is vital to life on Earth. It forms about 20 percent of Earth's atmosphere and it is used by living organisms to produce energy in a process called respiration.

QUADRICEPS
Muscles at the front of the legs that pull on the lower legs to straighten the knee.

SPONGY BONE
A type of bone tissue that is made from a lattice of bone with spaces in between. This helps to make larger bones strong, but light. The spaces are filled with bone marrow.

SYSTEMS
In the human body, these are collections of organs, tissues, and structures that perform a role. For example, nerves, the spinal cord, and the brain make up the nervous system.

TISSUES
A collection of similar cells that, together, carry out a particular function. For example, muscle tissue can contract to move parts of your body.

TRICEPS
The muscles on the backs of the upper arms, which pull on the lower arms to straighten the elbow.

VEINS
Blood vessels that carry blood toward the heart under low pressure. They have special valves inside them to stop blood from flowing the wrong way.

VERTEBRAE
The irregular-shaped bones that make up your spine. They have a hole in them through which the spinal cord runs from your pelvis to your brain.

X-RAY
A form of high-energy radiation that can pass through the soft tissues of the body, such as fat and muscle, but is absorbed by hard bones. Doctors use X-rays to take photos of the insides of our bodies to see if anything is damaged, such as a broken bone.

INDEX

3-D vision 45, 50

A
after images 60
air 28, 30
anus 27
appendicular skeleton 16
arms 22, 23

B
biceps 22
blind spots 49
blood 25, 31–35
blood cells 8, 15
blood vessels 28, 31
bone marrow 15
bones 15–20
brain 36–41, 42
breathing 25, 28–30
bronchi 28

C
calcium 15, 18
carbon dioxide 28, 31
cartilage 19
cells 8, 10
cerebellum 36
cerebrospinal fluid 37
cerebrum 36, 37
chyme 26, 27
circulatory system 9, 25, 31–5
cochlea 51
cornea 45

D
dermis 11
diaphragm 28, 29
digestive system 9, 25–7

E
ears 51–54
elbow 19
energy 25, 35
enzymes 25
epidermis 11
evaporation 12
exercise 24, 35
eyes 42, 45–50, 60

F
faces 38
fat 11
fingerprints 13, 14
flavors 55
food 25–27, 42, 56

G
gastric juices 26
genes 8

H
hair 9, 11, 12
hamstring 21
hearing 51–54
hearing aids 53
heart 21, 31–35
heartbeats 33
heat 12, 21, 24, 42

I
illusions 58
infection 31
intestines 25, 27

J
joints 15, 19, 20

K
knees 19, 21, 44

L
legs 21, 23
lenses 45, 46, 50
light 45, 47
light receptors 60
lungs 25, 28–30

M
memory 40
motor skills 39
muscles 9, 15, 21–4, 35

N
nerve cells 8, 38
neurons 36, 38, 44
nose 55, 56
nutrients 10, 25, 27, 31

O
optic nerve 45, 49
organs 8, 9, 15, 21
osmosis 10
ossicles 51
oxygen 25, 28, 31, 35

P
pheromones 55
pulse 35
pupils 45, 47

Q
quadriceps 21

R
reaction times 41
receptor cells 55
reflex reactions 44, 47, 61
respiratory system 9, 25, 28–30

S
saliva 25, 26
senses 42–61
sensors 11, 42, 43, 49
sight 42, 45–50, 60
skeleton 9, 15–20
skin 9, 11–14, 43, 44
skull 16, 37
smell 42, 55, 56
sound 51–54
sound waves 53
spine 16, 19, 44
stomach 25, 26
sweat 11, 12, 21, 24
systems 8–9

T
taste 42, 55, 56, 57
temperature 24, 44
tissues 8, 15, 17, 21
tongue 55
touch 42, 43, 60
triceps 22

V
valves 32, 33, 34
vertebrae 19
vibrations 51, 52
visual cortex 45
vital capacity 30

W
waste 25, 27, 31
water 10, 27

X
X-rays 17